Tyrannosaurus

Kimberley Jane Pryor

mc **Marshall Cavendish**
Benchmark
New York

This edition first published in 2012 in the United States of America by Marshall Cavendish Benchmark
An imprint of Marshall Cavendish Corporation

Website: www.marshallcavendish.us

This publication represents the opinions and views of the author based on Kimberley Jane Pryor's personal experience, knowledge, and research. The information in this book serves as a general guide only. The author and publisher have used their best efforts in preparing this book and disclaim liability rising directly and indirectly from the use and application of this book.

Other Marshall Cavendish Offices:
Marshall Cavendish International (Asia) Private Limited, 1 New Industrial Road, Singapore 536196 • Marshall Cavendish International (Thailand) Co Ltd. 253 Asoke, 12th Flr, Sukhumvit 21 Road, Klongtoey Nua, Wattana, Bangkok 10110, Thailand • Marshall Cavendish (Malaysia) Sdn Bhd, Times Subang, Lot 46, Subang Hi-Tech Industrial Park, Batu Tiga, 40000 Shah Alam, Selangor Darul Ehsan, Malaysia

Marshall Cavendish is a trademark of Times Publishing Limited

Library of Congress Cataloging-in-Publication Data

Pryor, Kimberley Jane.
  Tyrannosaurus rex / Kimberley Jane Pryor.
    p. cm. — (Discovering Dinosaurs)
  Summary: "Discusses the physical characteristics, time period, diet, and habitat of the Tyrannosaurus Rex" —Provided by publisher.
  Includes index.
  ISBN 978-1-60870-539-9
  1. Tyrannosaurus rex—Juvenile literature. I. Title.
  QE862.S3P794 2012
  567.912'9—dc22
                                    2010037189

First published in 2011 by
MACMILLAN EDUCATION AUSTRALIA PTY LTD
15–19 Claremont Street, South Yarra 3141

Visit our website at www.macmillan.com.au or go directly to www.macmillanlibrary.com.au

Associated companies and representatives throughout the world.

Publisher: Carmel Heron
Commissioning Editor: Niki Horin
Managing Editor: Vanessa Lanaway
Editor: Laura Jeanne Gobal
Proofreader: Helena Newton
Designer: Kerri Wilson (cover and text)
Page Layout: Pier Vido and Domenic Lauricella
Photo Researcher: Brendan Gallagher
Illustrator: Melissa Webb
Production Controller: Vanessa Johnson

Printed in China

Acknowledgments
The author and publisher are grateful to the following for permission to reproduce copyright material:

Photographs courtesy of: iStockphoto/Arpad Benedek, **9**; Photolibrary/Kim Steele, **8**; Shutterstock/ctpaul, **29**, /Colton Stiffler, **14**.

Background image of ripples on water © Shutterstock/ArchMan.

While every care has been taken to trace and acknowledge copyright, the publisher tenders their apologies for any accidental infringement where copyright has proved untraceable. They would be pleased to come to a suitable arrangement with the rightful owner in each case.

For Nick, Thomas, and Ashley

1 3 5 6 4 2

Contents

What Are Dinosaurs?   4

Dinosaur Groups   6

How Do We Know about Dinosaurs?   8

Meet Tyrannosaurus   10

What Did Tyrannosaurus Look Like?   12

The Skull and Senses of Tyrannosaurus   14

Tyrannosaurus Fossils   16

Where Did Tyrannosaurus Live?   18

What Did Tyrannosaurus Eat?   20

Predator or Prey?   22

How Did Tyrannosaurus Live?   24

Life Cycle of Tyrannosaurus   26

What Happened to Tyrannosaurus?   28

Names and Their Meanings   30

Glossary   31

Index   32

When a word is printed in **bold**, you can look up
its meaning in the glossary on page 31.

What Are Dinosaurs?

Dinosaurs (*dy-no-soars*) were **reptiles** that lived millions of years ago. They were different from other reptiles because their legs were directly under their bodies instead of to their sides like today's reptiles. Dinosaurs walked or ran on land.

At one time, there were more than 1,000 different kinds of dinosaurs.

Dinosaurs lived during a period of time called the Mesozoic (*mes-ah-zoh-ik*) Era. The Mesozoic Era is divided into the Triassic (*try-ass-ik*), Jurassic (*je-rass-ik*), and Cretaceous (*krah-tay-shahs*) periods.

This timeline shows the three different periods of the Mesozoic Era, when dinosaurs lived.

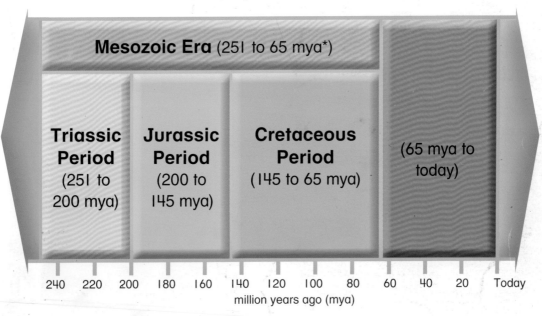

Mesozoic Era (251 to 65 mya*)

| **Triassic Period** (251 to 200 mya) | **Jurassic Period** (200 to 145 mya) | **Cretaceous Period** (145 to 65 mya) | (65 mya to today) |

240 220 200 180 160 140 120 100 80 60 40 20 Today

million years ago (mya)

*Note: mya = million years ago

Dinosaur Groups

Dinosaurs are sorted into two main groups according to their hipbones. Some dinosaurs had hipbones like a lizard's. Other dinosaurs had hipbones like a bird's.

All dinosaurs were either lizard-hipped or bird-hipped.

Dinosaurs

Lizard-hipped dinosaurs

Bird-hipped dinosaurs

Dinosaurs can be sorted into five smaller groups. Some lizard-hipped dinosaurs walked on two legs and ate meat. Others walked on four legs and ate plants. All bird-hipped dinosaurs ate plants.

Main Group	Smaller Group	Features	Examples
Lizard-hipped	Theropoda (*ther-ah-poh-dah*)	• Small to large • Walked on two legs • Meat-eaters	Tyrannosaurus Velociraptor
	Sauropodomorpha (*soar-rop-ah-dah-mor-fah*)	• Huge • Walked on four legs • Plant-eaters	Diplodocus
Bird-hipped	Thyreophora (*theer-ee-off-or-ah*)	• Small to large • Walked on four legs • Plant-eaters	Ankylosaurus
	Ornithopoda (*or-ni-thop-oh-dah*)	• Small to large • Walked on two or four legs • Plant-eaters	Muttaburrasaurus
	Ceratopsia (*ser-ah-top-see-ah*)	• Small to large • Walked on two or four legs • Plant-eaters • Frilled and horned skulls	Protoceratops

This table shows how dinosaurs can be sorted according to their size, how they walked, and the food they ate.

How Do We Know about Dinosaurs?

We know about dinosaurs because people have found fossils. Fossils are the preserved remains of plants and animals that lived long ago. They include bones, teeth, footprints, and eggs.

These dinosaur fossils are teeth that belonged to a Tyrannosaurus.

People who study fossils are called paleontologists (*pail-ee-on-tol-oh-jists*). They study fossils to learn about dinosaurs. They also remove dinosaur bones from rocks and rebuild **skeletons**.

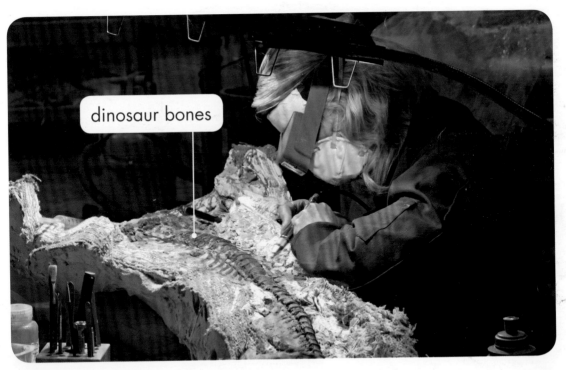

dinosaur bones

This paleontologist is carefully removing rock from dinosaur bones.

Meet Tyrannosaurus

Tyrannosaurus (*ty-ran-oh-soar-us*) was a large, lizard-hipped dinosaur. It belonged to a group of dinosaurs called theropoda. Dinosaurs in this group walked on two legs and ate meat.

Tyrannosaurus was a large, fierce dinosaur.

Tyrannosaurus lived in the late Cretaceous period, between 67 and 65 million years ago.

The purple area on this timeline shows when Tyrannosaurus lived.

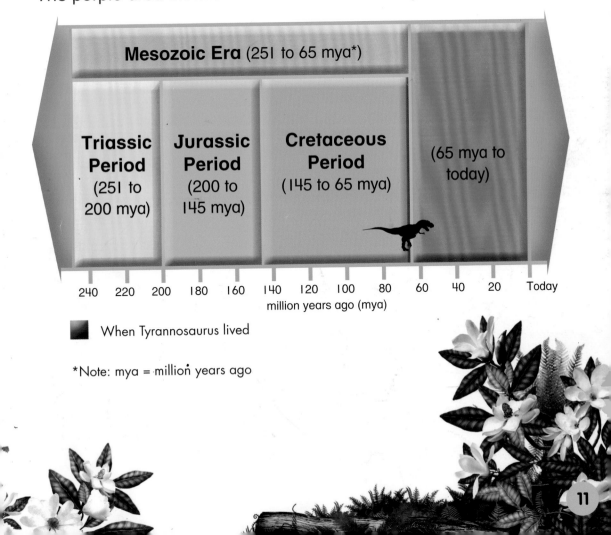

Mesozoic Era (251 to 65 mya*)

| **Triassic Period** (251 to 200 mya) | **Jurassic Period** (200 to 145 mya) | **Cretaceous Period** (145 to 65 mya) | (65 mya to today) |

240   220   200   180   160   140   120   100   80   60   40   20   Today
million years ago (mya)

■ When Tyrannosaurus lived

*Note: mya = million years ago

What Did Tyrannosaurus Look Like?

Tyrannosaurus was about 43 feet (13 meters) long and 13 feet (4 meters) tall at the hips. It weighed up to 7.7 tons (7 tonnes).

Tyrannosaurus was as tall as a two-story building and as heavy as an elephant!

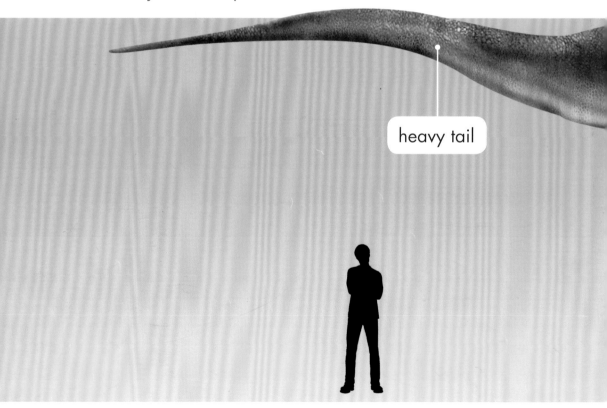

heavy tail

Tyrannosaurus walked on two legs. It had a large head, a heavy tail, and two tiny arms. Each arm had two claws on the end. Tyrannosaurus also had scaly skin.

large head

scaly skin

claws

tiny arms

legs

The Skull and Senses of Tyrannosaurus

Tyrannosaurus had a large skull and brain. This meant that it was smarter than most dinosaurs. Tyrannosaurus had powerful jaws with about sixty long, jagged teeth.

large skull

long, jagged teeth

powerful jaws

The largest Tyrannosaurus skull found is almost 5 feet (1.5 meters) in length!

Tyrannosaurus had a very good **sense** of smell. It could also see and hear well. Tyrannosaurus used these senses to help it find food.

The Senses of Tyrannosaurus				
Sense	Very Good	Good	Fair	Unable to Say
Sight		✔		
Hearing		✔		
Smell	✔			
Taste				✔
Touch				✔

Tyrannosaurus Fossils

Tyrannosaurus fossils have been found in the United States and Canada. They have also been found in Mongolia, in Asia.

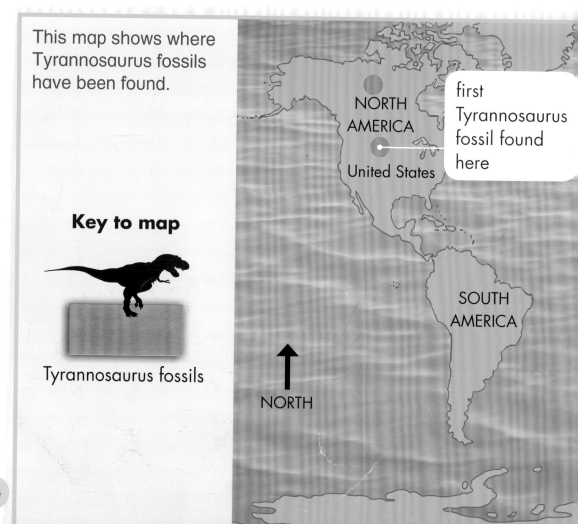

This map shows where Tyrannosaurus fossils have been found.

NORTH AMERICA

United States

first Tyrannosaurus fossil found here

Key to map

Tyrannosaurus fossils

SOUTH AMERICA

NORTH

In 1902, paleontologist Barnum Brown found the first Tyrannosaurus fossil in Montana. It was an entire skeleton. Many more fossils have been found since then.

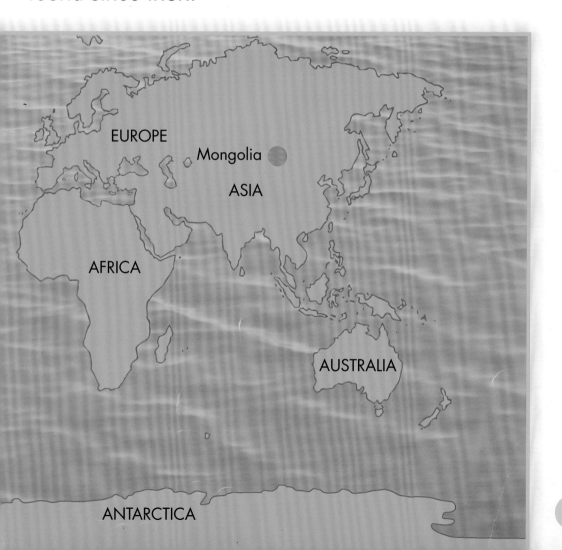

Where Did Tyrannosaurus Live?

Tyrannosaurus lived in forests near rivers and **swamps**. The forests were warm and damp.

Tyrannosaurus lived in forests where the trees were far apart, so it could move around easily.

conifers

The forests where Tyrannosaurus lived often had flowering plants, such as magnolias, and trees, such as conifers. There were other plants too, such as ferns and cycads.

ferns

cycads

magnolias

lichens

What Did Tyrannosaurus Eat?

Tyrannosaurus was a carnivore, or meat-eater. It ate large, plant-eating dinosaurs. Some of these dinosaurs were not very fast. This meant that Tyrannosaurus could sneak up and attack them.

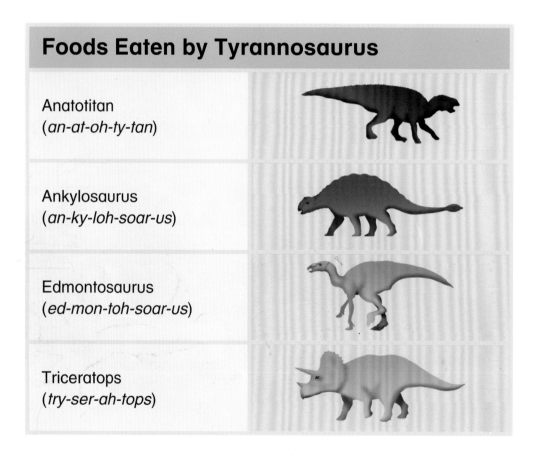

Foods Eaten by Tyrannosaurus

Anatotitan
(*an-at-oh-ty-tan*)

Ankylosaurus
(*an-ky-loh-soar-us*)

Edmontosaurus
(*ed-mon-toh-soar-us*)

Triceratops
(*try-ser-ah-tops*)

Paleontologists have different ideas about what kind of meat Tyrannosaurus ate. Many paleontologists think Tyrannosaurus caught and ate living animals. Some paleontologists think Tyrannosaurus found and ate dead animals.

Tyrannosaurus may have hunted living animals or dead ones.

Predator or Prey?

Many paleontologists think Tyrannosaurus was a powerful **predator**. They think it used its strong legs to run faster than its **prey**. Some paleontologists think Tyrannosaurus snuck up on its prey.

Tyrannosaurus took 16-foot-long (5-meters-long) **strides** when chasing its prey.

Once its prey was caught, Tyrannosaurus would sink its jagged teeth into it. Tyrannosaurus would then pull its head back, ripping away meat and bone.

The bite of Tyrannosaurus was eight times more powerful than a lion's bite!

How Did Tyrannosaurus Live?

Tyrannosaurus lived alone. Paleontologists know this because most Tyrannosaurus skeletons have been found many miles apart. Tyrannosaurus also guarded its hunting ground from other predators.

Tyrannosaurus lived and hunted alone, so it did not have to share its prey.

Tyrannosaurus spent its time resting and hunting for food. Males also spent time fighting other males and looking for females to **mate** with.

Male Tyrannosauruses often sank their teeth into each other when they were fighting.

Life Cycle of Tyrannosaurus

Paleontologists study fossils and living animals to learn about the life cycle of Tyrannosaurus.

1. An adult male Tyrannosaurus killed a prey animal to attract a female. The male and female mated.

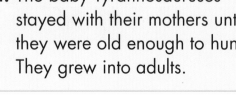

4. The baby Tyrannosauruses stayed with their mothers until they were old enough to hunt. They grew into adults.

They believe there were four main stages in the life cycle of Tyrannosaurus. This is what it may have been like.

2. The female laid several eggs in a nest. She covered the eggs with moss and lichen. She stayed near the nest to guard the eggs.

3. Baby Tyrannosauruses hatched from the eggs. Their mothers brought them meat to eat.

What Happened to Tyrannosaurus?

Tyrannosaurus became **extinct** about 65 million years ago. Many paleontologists think it died out when a large **meteorite** hit Earth. A meteorite would have caused most plants and animals to die.

1. A large meteorite hits Earth, causing dust clouds that block out the sun.

2. Plants get no sunshine and die.

3. Dinosaurs run out of food and die.

The meteorite impact would have caused dust clouds, which would have blocked out the sun.

Some paleontologists think Tyrannosaurus was dying out before the meteorite hit Earth. This is because Earth's **climate** was changing. Also, volcanoes were releasing **lava** and poisonous gases, which would have affected Tyrannosaurus.

Tyrannosaurus could not survive changing conditions on Earth, leaving us with only fossils.

Names and Their Meanings

Dinosaurs are named by people who discover them or paleontologists who study them. A dinosaur may be named for its appearance or behavior. Its name may also honor a person or place.

Name	Meaning
Dinosaur	Terrible lizard—because people thought dinosaurs were powerful lizards
Ankylosaurus	Fused lizard—because many of its bones were joined together
Diplodocus	Double beam—because it had special bones in its tail
Muttaburrasaurus	Muttaburra lizard—because it was discovered near the town of Muttaburra, in Australia
Protoceratops	First horned face—because it was one of the early horned dinosaurs
Tyrannosaurus	Tyrant lizard—because it was a fearsome ruler of the land
Velociraptor	Speedy thief—because it ran quickly and ate meat

Glossary

climate	The usual weather in a place.
extinct	No longer existing.
lava	The very hot, melted rock that flows out of a volcano.
lichens	Fungi growing together with plants called algae.
mate	Create offspring.
meteorite	A rock from space that has landed on Earth.
predator	An animal that hunts and kills other animals for food.
prey	An animal that is hunted and killed by other animals for food.
reptiles	Creeping or crawling animals that are covered with scales.
sense	A special ability that people and animals use to experience the world around them. Typically, those senses are sight, hearing, smell, taste, and touch.
skeletons	The bones inside the body of a person or an animal.
strides	Long steps taken when walking or running.
swamps	Areas of soft, wet ground.

Index

B

bird-hipped dinosaurs, 6, 7
brain, 14

C

carnivores, 20
claws, 13
Cretaceous period, 5, 11

E

eggs, 8, 27
extinction, 28, 29

F

food, 7, 15, 20, 21, 25, 28
forests, 18, 19
fossils, 8, 9, 16–17, 26, 29

J

Jurassic period, 5, 11

L

life cycle, 26–27
lizard-hipped dinosaurs, 6, 7, 10

M

meat-eating dinosaurs, 7, 10, 20, 21, 23, 27, 30
Mesozoic Era, 5, 11

P

paleontologists, 9, 17, 21, 22, 24, 26, 28, 29, 30
plant-eating dinosaurs, 7, 20
predators, 22, 24
prey, 22, 23, 24, 26

R

reptiles, 4

S

senses, 15
skeletons, 9, 17, 24
skin, 13
skulls, 7, 14

T

tail, 12, 13, 30
teeth, 8, 14, 23, 25
Triassic period, 5, 11